IMAGES
of America

ARDEN-ARCADE

T0279882

This is an aerial view of the upper region of Arden-Arcade in 1947. At center is the newly constructed Town & Country Village at the corner of Marconi and Fulton Avenues. In the background, tree-lined Arcade Creek acts as a border to McClellan Field. (Courtesy of Steve Anderson, Anderson Bros. Pharmacy.)

ON THE COVER: This c. 1955 photograph shows the Arcade Fire Department hosting Fire Prevention Week at Town & Country Village. During this time, the department was predominately staffed by community volunteers, with a dozen full-time paid staff. The first dispatchers were Mr. and Mrs. John Mantzouranis. They had a store at the corner of Auburn Boulevard and Morse Avenue, and above the store was their home. When a resident called with an emergency, one of them would answer the call. (Courtesy of Pioneer Mutual Hook and Ladder Society.)

IMAGES
of America

ARDEN-ARCADE

Colette Kavanaugh

ARCADIA
PUBLISHING

Copyright © 2023 by Colette Kavanaugh
ISBN 978-1-4671-6001-8

Published by Arcadia Publishing
Charleston, South Carolina

Printed in the United States of America

Library of Congress Control Number: 2023937925

For all general information, please contact Arcadia Publishing:
Telephone 843-853-2070
Fax 843-853-0044
E-mail sales@arcadiapublishing.com
For customer service and orders:
Toll-Free 1-888-313-2665

Visit us on the Internet at www.arcadiapublishing.com

To the past, present, and future residents of Arden-Arcade.

CONTENTS

ACKNOWLEDGMENTS

This book would not have been possible without the generosity of time and spirit from the following: Melinda Alberti Jung, Mary Anagnostopoulos, Steven Anderson of Anderson Bros. Pharmacy, Stefani L. Baldivia of Meriam Library at California State University Chico, Bancroft Library at University of Berkeley, Stephanie Barden, Steve Biondi, Donald Cox, Ronald Cole, Sara Cordes of the California State Library, Mark Dolislager of Arden Hills, Jim Eastman and Rev. Roger Jones of the Unitarian Universalist Society of Sacramento, Ingrid Foster of the Sacramento Country Day School, Susan Henas, Eugene Hepting, Teresa and Craig Higgins of Chocolate Confections, Caleb Andrew Hinsley of Sacramento Public Library, Swami Isha of the Vedanta Society, Dan Jensen, Ryan Koledin, Terri Meyer and Brian Lawrence of Emigh Hardware, Patricia Moran, David Munger of Sacramento Public Library, Don Murphy and Ric Williams, Nancy O'Connor, Nicholas Pointek of the Center of Sacramento History, Max Schlesinger of Sam's Hof Brau, James Scott of the Sacramento Room at Sacramento Public Library, Monica Stark of Valcom News, Gretchen Steinberg, Kathy Stricklin, Joan S. Tully of Arden Middle School, Raquel Urbani of Dreyfuss + Blackford, Debbie Viramontes, Bette Waterstreet, Herb E. Winterstein, Randy Wootton of Metro Fire, and Yosemite National Park Archives.

Thank you to everyone at Arcadia Publishing for this opportunity and for inviting me to do this book. Shout out of thanks to my editors Erin Vosgien, Jim Kempert, and Stacia Bannerman.

Extra special thanks to Liz G. Fisher, Melanie Knight, Crissanka Christadoss, Connie Nicely (thanks, Mom!), Martha Zarate, and my clients at Colibrí Electrology for listening to me drone on about Arden-Arcade's history.

Extra, extra special thanks go to my partner and favorite research assistant, Dylan Kavanaugh. Your support and encouragement astound me.

Please forgive me if I forgot anyone in my haste.

INTRODUCTION

Change is constant. Evolution is inevitable. Arden-Arcade is no exception to this rule of life. For nearly 14,000 years, the land was occupied by the Valley Nisenan, Southern Maidu, and Miwok indigenous people. They had villages dotted throughout the landscape filled with languages, music, and customs. Once the European settlers arrived, specifically in the Gold Rush of 1849, a major shift occurred. Disease among the indigenous people, the loss of life-sustaining resources, and the forceful removal of lands once called home all but eradicated these thriving societies. Arden-Arcade's history, like all American communities, possesses painful pasts.

During this struggle of change, the Rancho Del Paso took shape through a land grant between John Augustus Sutter and Mexican governor Juan Bautista Alvarado. However, the validity of this grant was debatable, as it appeared more of an assumption of ownership on Sutter's part. Therefore, Eliab Grimes, along with his brother Hiram Grimes, and John Sinclair formally petitioned the new governor, Manuel Micheltorena, to ensure the land ownership was on the level. Micheltorena officially approved the petition on December 20, 1844. Grimes owned the rancho until 1849.

Eventually, the Rancho Del Paso landed in the hands of the wealthy elite brothers-in-law James Ben Ali Haggin and Lloyd Tevis. Both men were attorneys and entrepreneurs. Haggin became well known in the horse racing world due to his well-bred champion racehorses. This notoriety gave the Rancho Del Paso exposure. The name Arcade was used to describe Haggin's ranch, as it had a row of valley oak trees in a formation reminiscent of an architectural arcade.

Haggin and Tevis sold the Rancho Del Paso to the Sacramento Valley Colonization Company in 1910. The company was owned by Orlando Robertson. The name Arden originates from Robertson's hometown of Arden Hills, Minnesota. Robertson was responsible for many of the street names of the Arden-Arcade area, specifically Bell Street, Edison Avenue, Fulton Avenue, Howe Avenue, Marconi Avenue, Morse Avenue, Whitney Avenue, and Watt Avenue, which he named after famous inventors.

The Sacramento Valley Colonization Company used real estate firms to sell tracts of land to develop the area as an agricultural community. Given the favorable mild climate, ample water resources, and fertile soil due to the American River, it was easy to advertise the land. One of the main real estate companies was the Ben Leonard Company, which created an attractive brochure boasting the area's resources, calling it the "Pasadena of Northern California," which was predominately the area around Arcade Park. With the construction of Pacific Air Depot (later McClellan Air Force Base), the area began to see a shift from agriculture to sprawling suburbia. The air field was built in 1935, and new residential areas began to spring up nearby. Architect and developer Jeré Strizek, living in Tracy, California, during this time, took note of this change and decided to build his own residential communities in the area. Shortly after, he started constructing Bohemian Village, along with his business partner, architect John W. Davis.

Strizek noticed that his new homes were not selling as quickly as they did in Tracy, due to a lack of access to goods and services in the immediate area. He purchased 11 acres at the corner of Fulton and Marconi Avenues, and with the assistance of Davis, the Town & Country Village shopping center was born in 1946.

Town & Country Village was one of the first shopping malls west of the Mississippi. It gained national attention not only for its variety of stores, but also for its unique design and shopping experience. Town & Country Village helped usher in the building boom of the post–World War II era in Arden-Arcade. Soon other local entrepreneurs would further push development in the area, such as the Kassis family, owners of the local Stop-N-Shop supermarket chain, who were instrumental in the construction of the Arden Fair shopping center along with developers Philip F. Heraty and William Gannon. The Kassis family also invested in Country Club Plaza and the iconic Country Club Lanes bowling alley.

The growth of the retail industry and the close proximity to downtown Sacramento brought fervent residential development to Arden-Arcade. Young families flocked to purchase the affordable homes from Jeré Strizek, Streng Bros., Wright and Kimbrough, and Randolph Parks. Along with the new residents, places of worship moved into the community, as did schools, libraries, and recreational activities.

Arden-Arcade soon transitioned from a cow town to a center of commerce. Country roads became known for business. Fulton Avenue became synonymous with the automobile, as Arden Way did with Arden Fair. Once Tower Records opened on Watt Avenue, it would be forever cemented in music history. Tower Records created a cultural phenomenon. The youth of the 1960s through the late 1990s were deeply connected with the store, as it helped define and perpetuate pop culture during its reign.

Through it all, the Arden-Arcade community has cultivated a distinctive identity and attracted an incredibly diverse population of more than 90,000 residents today. The community has been affected by economic recessions and lost many of its specialty shops and fondly remembered restaurants. Country Club Centre, once full of stores, has been mostly vacant for several years except for See's Candy, which has remained open since the 1950s. However, there are signs of new life moving into the vacant spaces. The community continues to evolve. Arden-Arcade's boundaries have been reduced slightly after portions were annexed by the City of Sacramento. California Exposition was annexed in 1959, the Arden Fair area in 1961, Haggin Oaks Golf Course up to Del Paso Regional Park in 1963, and Horst Ranch, also known as the Campus Commons area, in 1965. Ardent Arden-Arcade supporters attempted to incorporate the area into its own city in 2010, which would allow the area to have its own representation. Although the measure did not succeed, passionate residents continue to work tirelessly to advocate for their community and work to preserve and protect the last remaining Googie and Mid-century Modern buildings from destruction.

As the digital age continues, it will be interesting to see how the commerce side of Arden-Arcade evolves with the times. History has shown that this community has a pattern of gaining notoriety for innovation, be it horse breeding or shopping centers. What will be the next innovation that will come out of Arden-Arcade to make history? Perhaps a look back in time will leave some clues and provide a reminder of what makes this community so special.

One

THIS LAND WAS
THEIR LAND

Arden-Arcade was home to the Valley Nisenan tribe for centuries. The land that this community resides on first belonged to them. Before European settlers arrived, the area was rich with antelope, elk, grasshoppers, and grizzly bears. Grizzles would travel in packs of 60 around the American River.

Once European settlers arrived, the way of life for the Nisenan changed dramatically. Disease had tragic consequences for many California Indians, often wiping out entire villages. The mission period in the 18th and 19th centuries further displaced and disrupted native villages as missionaries claimed land and attempted to eradicate native culture by converting native people to Catholicism. The Gold Rush of 1849 brought even more disease and destruction to native communities. The population of the native communities was reduced by 90 percent in less than 50 years.

The Valley Nisenan had numerous villages throughout the Sacramento area. Most notable were the villages of Pushune and Kadema. Pushune was in Discovery Park, along the confluence of the Sacramento River and American River near downtown Sacramento, and Kadema was in Arden-Arcade by Watt Avenue and the American River just south of Fair Oaks Boulevard. Kadema was quite large and extended up past modern-day Jesuit High School. Scholars believe the village of Kadema had been around since 300 A.D. and had residents until 1930. Its peak population was about 500 residents.

In 1960, the village and cemetery were excavated to make way for a housing development. The developer named the neighboring street Kadema Drive to memorialize the village so the name would not be forgotten.

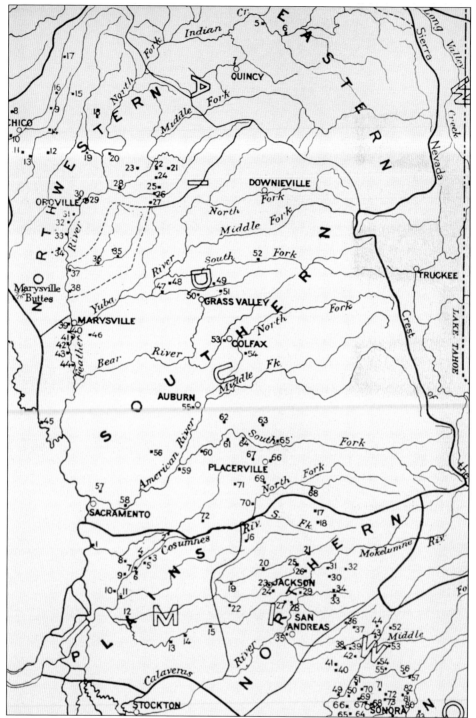

This map from 1925 by Alfred Kroeber shows California Indian villages throughout the central valley and Sierra foothills. The numbers on the map represent villages. Nos. 57 and 58, along the American River, are the villages of Pushune and Kadema. (Courtesy of Meriam Library, California State University, Chico.)

The Nisenan tribe utilized sweathouses and a dance house within their village for ceremonial and spiritual practices. Dance houses were known as Kum. This image of a sweathouse is from 1911. (Courtesy of the Center of Sacramento History.)

Figure 42.—Woman pounding acorns.

This illustration shows a Nisenan woman pounding acorns to make acorn mash. Acorns were about 80 percent of the Nisenan diet. They were gathered daily and dried for up to a year before they were processed and cooked. Processing included breaking the shell and then grinding and pounding the acorn into a fine flour. (Courtesy of Meriam Library, California State University, Chico.)

This illustration by Henry Brown drawn around 1852 depicts two Valley Nisenan women. One is carrying a baby in a papoose and the other is carrying baskets. The Nisenan were known for their expertly woven baskets. They were watertight and used for gathering, cooking, and storing goods. (Courtesy of Bancroft Library, University of Berkeley.)

Nisenan "Blind Tom" Cleanso is pictured in 1925. He was called "Blind Tom" because he was born blind. Cleanso was the last caretaker, bead maker, and Nisenan inhabitant of Kadema. He passed away in 1930. (Courtesy of Bancroft Library, University of Berkeley.)

Although legally blind, Tom Cleanso was known for his bead and abalone shell work. These four shells were found in his cabin after his death in 1932. Abalone shells were worn for ceremonies such as dances. (Courtesy of Yosemite National Park Archives.)

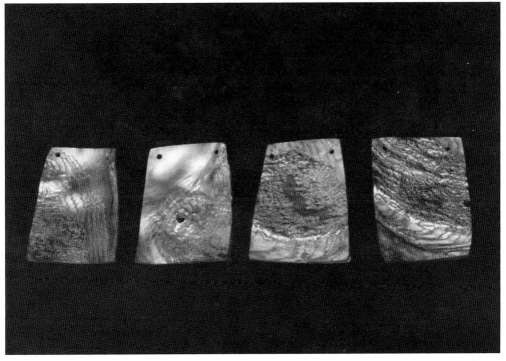

Tom Cleanso was originally born in the Nisenan village of Pushune at the confluence of the Sacramento and American Rivers. He provided valuable history and information to Alfred Kroeber, who wrote *The Valley Nisenan* in 1929. (Courtesy of Bancroft Library, University of Berkeley.)

Seen here are Capt. Mike Cleanso and his wife, Dolores. Captain Cleanso was recruited, along with other Kadema residents, to work for John Augustus Sutter at New Helvetia. (Courtesy of California State Library.)

Capt. Mike Cleanso, born in 1821, was the last headman of the village of Kadema. During the excavation of Kadema, former resident Lillie Williams told how she and Captain Cleanso would walk all the way to the coast with burden baskets full of acorns to trade with the coastal people for abalone shells. (Courtesy of California State Library.)

The cemetery in Kadema is seen here in 1942. Those known to be buried here are Capt. Mike Cleanso, John K. Cook, Tom Cleanso, Lillie Cook, and Ellen Adams. Lillie and Ellen were both children. This cemetery was excavated in February 1960. (Photograph by Eugene Hepting, courtesy of the Center of Sacramento History.)

Archaeologist John S. Clemmer is seen at the Kadema village site. In January 1960, the Nisenan village was excavated to make way for housing developments in Sierra Oaks. Large pits were dug to unearth artifacts, and information was cataloged for educational and historical purposes. (Courtesy of the Center of Sacramento History.)

John S. Clemmer is seen here unearthing more artifacts at Kadema. The pottery shown in the photograph was likely obtained by the Nisenan through trade, since they did not make pottery. Clemmer and his group of volunteers, with the aid of former Kadema resident Lillie Williams, worked tirelessly to uncover and catalog the artifacts while defending the site from rampant vandalism. (Courtesy of the Center of Sacramento History.)

Two

RANCHO DEL PASO

On June 18, 1841, John Augustus Sutter was deeded the New Helvetia land grant by Mexican governor Juan Bautista Alvarado. This land included the city of Sacramento, Sutter, and Yolo counties. Technically, the land on which Arden-Arcade resides was not part of the New Helvetian deed, but Sutter claimed the land anyway. On August 10, 1843, he deeded the land to Eliab Grimes, Hiram Grimes, and John Sinclair to pay for supplies for Sutter Fort. This was the birth of Rancho Del Paso. The name means "Ranch of the Pass," which referred to the ford on the American River near the present-day H Street bridge.

The Grimes brothers and Sinclair, suspicious about the validity of the deed, petitioned the new governor, Manuel Micheltorena, who officially approved their petition on December 20, 1844. Both Eliab Grimes and John Sinclair would remain on the rancho until 1849.

The rancho's next owner was Samuel Norris, who was most known for obtaining a US patent on the land and establishing legal ownership. This was a costly endeavor; however, on May 4, 1858, Pres. James Buchanan recognized the Mexican land grant and confirmed Norris as the legal owner. Norris's attorneys for this process were James Ben Ali Haggin and Lloyd Tevis, the rancho's next owners. Norris was a very litigious man. He was known to sue anyone for just about anything, which eventually got the best of him. Due to mounting legal debts, he lost Rancho Del Paso. It went up for public auction, and Haggin and Tevis swooped in and purchased the land for $63,500.

Haggin and Tevis owned Rancho Del Paso from 1862 to 1910. By 1886, the rancho was known nationally for racehorses due to Haggin's skilled trainer John Mackey. In 1910, Haggin and Tevis sold Rancho Del Paso for $1.5 million to the Sacramento Valley Colonization Company, changing the trajectory of the area from a large rancho to a rural community.

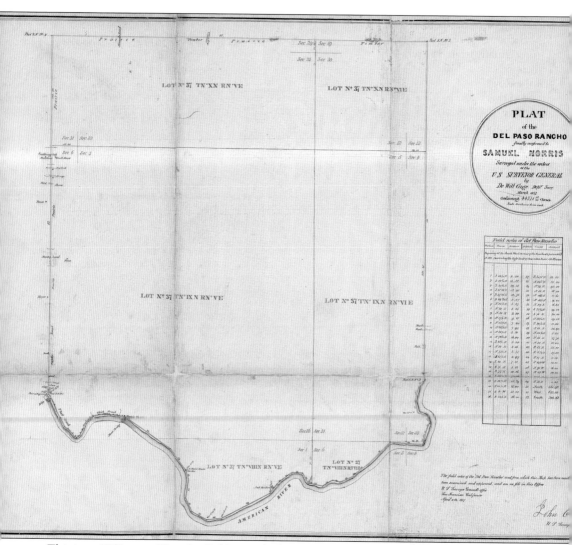

This is an 1857 map of Rancho Del Paso. The landowner at the time was Samuel Norris, and locals called the land "Norris Ranch." Norris developed a town called Norris Town near the American River; however, it was abandoned after major flooding. An interesting fact is that the residents of Norristown did not vote for Norris to be mayor of his own town. (Courtesy of the Center of Sacramento History.)

John Augustus Sutter arrived in the Sacramento region in 1839. He was originally from Switzerland, where he claimed he was a captain of the Royal Swiss Guard. Sutter deeded the Rancho Del Paso property to Eliab Grimes, Hiram Grimes, and John Sinclair on August 10, 1843. (Courtesy of the California State Library.)

Manuel Micheltorena was governor of Mexican California from 1842 to 1845. He officially deeded Rancho Del Paso to Eliab Grimes, as Grimes did not fully trust the deed from Sutter. (Courtesy of the Bancroft Library, University of Berkeley.)

Samuel Norris was originally from Denmark. His birth name was Gotthilf Wilhelm Becher Christensen. Norris was very litigious. Even after he lost Rancho Del Paso due to legal debts, he attempted to sue James Ben Ali Haggin and Lloyd Tevis, claiming they manipulated him into losing his land. (Courtesy of the California State Library.)

Samuel Brannan owned Rancho Del Paso for three months in 1851, and then sold it back to Norris. Brannan started California's first newspaper, and when gold was discovered, he managed to set up a general store at Sutter's Fort before announcing the discovery in his paper. This advantageous move made him California's first millionaire. However, Brannan's excessive and extravagant lifestyle drained his assets by 1880. He spent his remaining years living in a tent in Escondido. (Courtesy of the California State Library.)

James Ben Ali Haggin was an astute businessman and attorney from Kentucky. In his lifetime, he acquired around 400,000 acres of land in California and other states in the West. Haggin is most known for his champion racehorses, which won 37 races in 1886, and 71 in 1887. (Courtesy of the Bancroft Library, University of Berkeley.)

Lloyd Tevis, like Haggin, was also from Kentucky and an astute businessman and attorney. He made his fortune in real estate, mining, law, and water rights. Additionally, he was president of Wells Fargo at one time. Tevis owned half of Rancho Del Paso. (Courtesy of the Bancroft Library, University of Berkeley.)

The lower region of Haggin Ranch just off Fair Oaks Boulevard is seen here in 1944 looking toward the American River. (Photograph by Eugene Hepting, courtesy of the Center of Sacramento History.)

This 1942 photograph shows barns near Jesuit High School on Fair Oaks Boulevard. Up to 60 racehorses were kept here on Haggin Ranch. This is where they were trained and reared. (Photograph by Eugene Hepting, courtesy of the Center of Sacramento History.)

According to local historian Eugene Hepting, this was the home of two Nisenan who James Ben Ali Haggin could not drive off the land. They were born at Kadema, and even though these barns were erected in their village, they refused to leave. The Indians never left the property, and were buried in the cemetery at Kadema. (Photograph by Eugene Hepting, courtesy of the Center of Sacramento History.)

This was the barn where "special oats" were crushed for the Haggin's racehorses. The oats were grown nearby in favorable conditions. (Photograph by Eugene Hepting, courtesy of the Center of Sacramento History.)

These Haggin Ranch barns were in an area that became the Sierra Dairy Farm. (Photograph by Eugene Hepting, courtesy of the Center of Sacramento History.)

This mid-1860s stereograph image shows the Central Pacific Railroad headed toward North Arden Way. James Ben Ali Haggin built a railroad at Marconi Avenue and Auburn Boulevard to efficiently ship his racehorses all over the nation. Near the station were 24 barns with up to 64 horse stalls. This was the ranch's shipping and sales center. (Courtesy of California State Library.)

John Mackey was superintendent of Rancho Del Paso and was incredibly skilled at training champion horses. Mackey worked at the rancho for over 30 years, and when the horses were shipped to auctions in New York, he would accompany them on the train. (Courtesy of California State Library.)

The superintendent's house in the lower portion of Haggin Ranch is seen here in 1944. (Photograph by Eugene Hepting, courtesy of the Center of Sacramento History.)

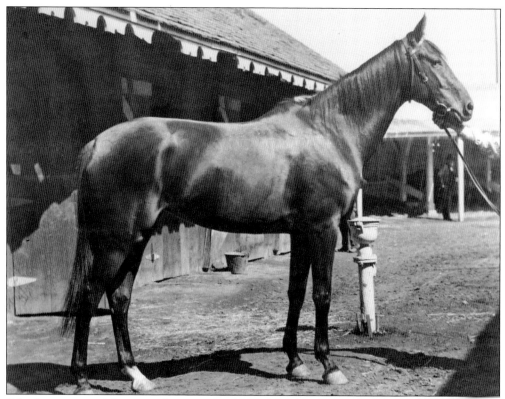

Salvador was one of the many champion racehorses raised at Rancho Del Paso. Salvador was a big earner, winning over 16 races. Most notably, in 1890, he set a record at Monmouth Park that stood for 28 years. (Courtesy of the Center of Sacramento History.)

This 1944 photograph shows a derelict building crumbling on Haggin Ranch. This is near the lowlands by the American River. Just beyond the ruins was a racetrack where Mackey would train the horses. (Photograph by Eugene Hepting, courtesy of the Center of Sacramento History.)

Three

THE PASADENA OF NORTHERN CALIFORNIA

In 1910, Arden-Arcade was very rural. In an effort to sell the land to prospective farmers and homesteaders, real estate advertisers pitched the Arcade Park area of Arden-Arcade as the "Pasadena of Northern California" or the "Cream of the Haggin Grant," due to its rich soil and Mediterranean climate.

Additionally, the location of Arcade Park in proximity to Sacramento was ideal for transportation. Before automobiles, trains and steamboats were the quickest modes of transport. However, a horse and buggy could make the short trip to the city in a reasonable time.

One of the main real estate brokers to sell Arcade Park was the Ben Leonard Company, owned and operated by Ben Leonard. His company purchased 1,600 acres of Rancho Del Paso in 1911 and coined the "Pasadena of Northern California" slogan. As the land was developed for farms, it was only a matter of time before businesses would move to be closer to their customers, turning Arcade from a rural community into a burgeoning town.

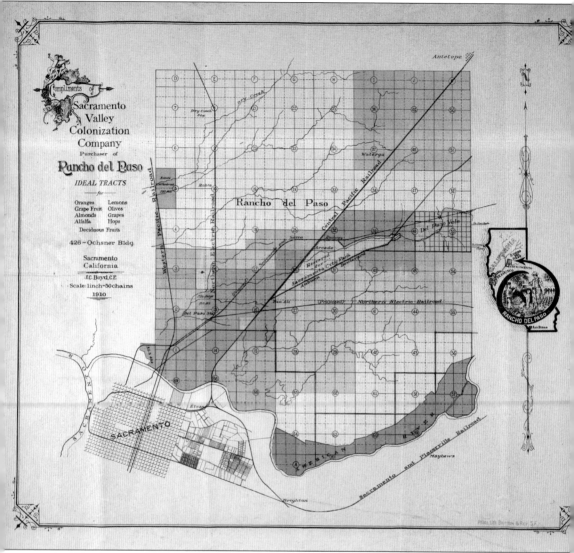

In 1910, the Sacramento Valley Colonization Company purchased Rancho Del Paso for $1.5 million. This map shows the ideal tracts on which to grow oranges, grapefruit, olives, hops, and more. Note the proposed Northern Electric Railroad on the map, which was about where El Camino and Marconi Avenues are today. (Courtesy of California State Library.)

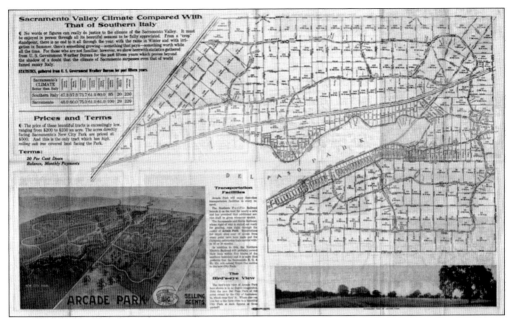

Seen here is a map of the available tracts of land for sale by the Ben Leonard Company. This map came in a brochure created by the company in 1912 and includes a comparison chart of the climate in southern Italy to Arcade to show how optimal the area was to grow fruits, vegetables, and flowers. (Courtesy of California State Library.)

Auburn Highway, now Auburn Boulevard, meanders by Del Paso Park in 1937. Del Paso Park officially opened in April 1911; not long after, the land surrounding the park was sold as premium farmland. (Courtesy of Sacramento Room, Sacramento Public Library.)

A TYPICAL CALIFORNIA POULTRY FARM, NEAR ARCADE PARK

TRACT NO. 12 IN ARCADE PARK, CONTAINING 8 12-100 ACRES AT $250 PER ACRE

Seen here are additional images from the Ben Leonard Company Arcade Park brochure. The top image shows a quite substantial free-range poultry farm, and the bottom shows available acreage. Note the price of $250 per acre. (Courtesy of California State Library.)

This is an aerial photograph from 1933 of a Spanish-style villa at 3001 Morse Avenue. In the foreground is the Del Paso Country Club. Well-known Nevada singer Harriet Ede Pendergast lived in this home until her death in 1947. (Courtesy of the Center of Sacramento History.)

This view of wide open spaces was captured on Cottage Way looking down Fulton Avenue toward Marconi Avenue in 1947. (Photograph by Eugene Hepting, courtesy of the Center of Sacramento History.)

Fulton Avenue heading toward Marconi Avenue is seen here in 1947 with a farm on the right. In 1928, the County of Sacramento decided to pave Fulton Avenue along with one mile of the east end of Marconi Avenue, which was known as Country Club Road at the time. (Photograph by Eugene Hepting, courtesy of the Center of Sacramento History.)

This c. 1943 photograph shows Ronald Cole's family farm on Route 7, which later become Bell Street. Looking toward the tree nearest the water would be what is now the intersection of Cottage Way and Howe Avenue. From left to right are Ronald's bulldog Spot; David Rose, whose parents owned the farm, which later became Tiny Tots Pre School; Russel Hutchinson; Forest Burton; Ray Cole (on the bike in front of Forest), Ronald's brother; and Ron, wearing an aviator's cap, which was very popular during those World War II days. (Courtesy of Ronald Cole.)

Ronald Cole's mother, Elva L. Cole, poses on the family farm. Behind her is the intersection of Bell Street and Cottage Way. The telephone poles are along Cottage Way. The open field is the future site of Jeré Strizek's flat-top housing. (Courtesy of Ronald Cole.)

This photograph shows the Park Hill Estates neighborhood with a recently built home. This neighborhood is located between Fulton Avenue and Watt Avenue with the cross streets of Cottage Way and El Camino Avenue. (Photograph by Eugene Hepting, courtesy of the Center of Sacramento History.)

New homes are being advertised for Del Paso Manor, between Watt and Eastern Avenues with the cross streets of El Camino and Marconi Avenues. Gradually, the once-rural community was transitioning to 1950s suburbia. (Photograph by Eugene Hepting, courtesy of the Center of Sacramento History.)

Four

JERÉ STRIZEK WELCOMES YOU

Architect and developer Jeré Strizek seized an opportunity that would forever change the trajectory of the Arden-Arcade area and led to the legendary development boom of the 1950s. Strizek's family originated from historic Bohemia, which is now part of the Czech Republic. Strizek's family emigrated to America and settled in Seattle, Washington, where he completed his architecture degree. Eventually, Strizek made his way to California. First, he became known in Tracy, California, for his unique and affordable flat-top, two-bedroom, one-bath homes. Strizek's homes were very popular, and in the 1930s, he began to look at Sacramento as a development opportunity. In 1935, Pacific Air Depot, later McClellan Air Force Base, was built, and residential homes began to spring up in the Arden-Arcade community. Strizek purchased lots and started to build homes in Bohemian Village, named as a nod to his homeland. During this time, the closest shopping options were in downtown Sacramento on K Street. Strizek saw another opportunity. For $280 an acre, he purchased an 11-acre plot on the corners of Fulton and Marconi Avenues, which was once an Arabian horse farm. Strizek and his business partner, architect John W. Davis, developed Town & Country Village, which officially opened in September 1946. A first of its kind in the United States, the shopping center offered over 60 specialty shops along with ample parking. What made Town & Country Village so distinctive was it offered shoppers an experience: the open-air walkways covered in lush ivy, tropical gardens, and kitschy Western décor.

Additionally, the shops were independently operated. Strizek avoided national chains, perhaps to preserve the vision he had for the space, or just to support local business owners. Regardless, Town & Country Village became a destination and a national tourist attraction. Strizek was a visionary and community builder, and soon, Arden-Arcade went from a growing town to a bustling economic force.

This c. 1947 aerial photograph shows Town & Country Village before construction of the Village Theater in 1949. Town & Country Village is on the northeast corner of Fulton and Marconi Avenues. Built in 1945 by developer Jeré Strizek, it officially opened in 1946. (Courtesy of Steve Anderson, Anderson Bros. Pharmacy.)

Here is a closer look at Town & Country Village from the air in 1947. When the shopping center opened, it quickly became one of the customary tourist attractions in the area. Families with visiting relatives would often take them to see Sutter's Fort, Crocker Art Gallery, the state capitol, and Town & Country Village. (Courtesy of Sacramento Room, Sacramento Public Library.)

New construction is pictured along Fulton Avenue in 1947. Town & Country Village attracted other entrepreneurs to the area. Fulton Avenue was created by Sacramento County decades earlier to help with traffic flow to downtown. This proved to be advantageous for future business. (Photograph by Eugene Hepting, courtesy of the Center of Sacramento History.)

A young woman poses in front of the main corridor of Town & Country Village in 1955. Jeré Strizek designed the shopping center in an early California pioneer motif with Mission-styled buildings and a Western flair. (Author's collection.)

Seen here in 1948, Town & Country Village was built from old bridge timbers, which Strizek sourced from the Central Pacific Railroad. He also purchased weathered telephone poles from the Pacific Telephone Company to give a rustic look and feel to the shopping center. (Courtesy of Sacramento Room, Sacramento Public Library.)

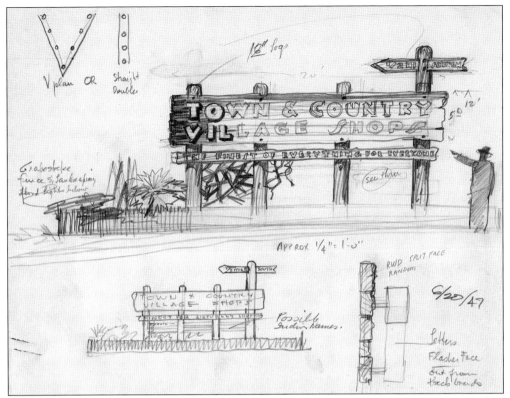

Architect John W. Davis sketched the Town & Country Village sign in 1947. Various design ideas are shown, with measurements. Davis worked with Jeré Strizek for many years designing Town & Country Village and homes in the area. (Courtesy of Sacramento Room, Sacramento Public Library.)

This was the first building constructed for Town & Country Village, in 1946. It was toward the back of the shopping center on Marconi Avenue separate from the main shopping area, where the Sprouts Farmers Market parking lot is today. Note the chimney on the side of the building. (Courtesy of Sacramento Room, Sacramento Public Library.)

Casual Corner and Mommy Mode stores in Town & Country Village are seen here. Tropical gardens filled the corridors. Note the cacti in pots near the store entryways. (Courtesy of Sacramento Room, Sacramento Public Library.)

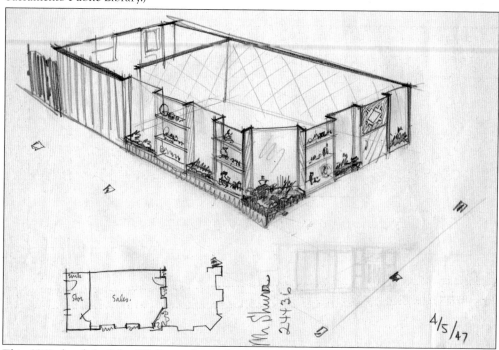

This 1947 sketch by John W. Davis shows the design of the May Shurr Antiques store in Town & Country Village. The design shows built-in display windows, which were ultimately included. Several residents remember looking at random old relics in those windows. (Courtesy of Sacramento Room, Sacramento Public Library.)

Clair & Daley, seen here around 1948, was on the Fulton Avenue side of the shopping center and was owned and operated by Marie Daley and Florence Clair. Their store offered women a "desirable, well-groomed look without exorbitant prices." (Courtesy of Sacramento Room, Sacramento Public Library.)

As seen in the late 1940s, the open-air corridors were lined with semi-tropical plants. Note the hanging potted pots. The design of Town & Country Village gave the shopping center national recognition, and it became a tourist attraction. (Courtesy of Sacramento Room, Sacramento Public Library.)

This is the Adobe Court and Village Flower Shop. Jeré Strizek forbade the use of electrical signs and avoided relationships with nationally known chains to maintain a unique shopping experience and support independent stores. (Courtesy of Sacramento Room, Sacramento Public Library.)

More Old West charm is pictured here, with wagon wheels sourced from Oregon. Strizek used old materials to cut down on the cost of building the shopping center. Town & Country Village gave shoppers more than just stores to purchase goods; it gave them a leisurely shopping experience. (Author's collection.)

The Town & Country Village sign frames the Village Theater and filling station in the background. This 1950s view is looking northeast from Marconi Avenue toward Fulton Avenue. (Courtesy of Sacramento Room, Sacramento Public Library.)

The Village Theater officially opened on July 1, 1949, with the movies *Red Canyon* and *The Little Witch*. The theater was owned and operated by John Harvey. (Courtesy of the Center of Sacramento History.)

The Village Theater had one screen and 903 seats made by Heywood Wakefield. They were spring loge chairs that had the ability to rock and were considered premium chairs. (Courtesy of Sacramento Room, Sacramento Public Library.)

In its heyday, the Village Theater was one of Sacramento's premiere movie houses. It closed in 1985 and became a bingo hall. The theater was razed in 2006. (Courtesy of Sacramento Room, Sacramento Public Library.)

On a typical busy day in 1953, parking lots on either side of Fulton Avenue are full. At right, the Village Theater is playing *Blowing Wind* starring Gary Cooper and Barbara Stanwyck, and *Vice Squad* with Paulette Goodard.

Aldo's was a high-end restaurant in Town & Country Village known for its continental cuisine and live music. Local pianist Mario R. Ferrari serenaded customers with beautiful melodies. He could play just about any song request and was always decked out in a tuxedo. He played at Aldo's for many years, adding to the elegant ambiance. (Author's collection.)

Aldo's was owned by Aldo Bovero (left) and Paul Coulat (right). It was a special place to celebrate birthdays, anniversaries, or engagements. Town & Country Village store Miles-N-Miles would often have fashion shows in the restaurant. Aldo's opened in 1965 and closed in 1999. (Courtesy of the Center of Sacramento History.)

Jeré Strizek (far right) hosts a luncheon at the Chuck Wagon in Town & Country Village for the student officers of Mather Field in 1949. From left to right are 1st Lt. Roy D. Leavitt, the base's public information officer; Brig. Gen. Carl Brown McDaniel; his wife Ruth McDaniel; and Strizek. (Courtesy of Sacramento Room, Sacramento Public Library.)

SACRAMENTO
FREE PUBLIC

Located on the 2700 block of Marconi Avenue, Cardinal grocery store opened at Town & Country Village in 1950. Cardinal was a homegrown chain store and remained at Town & Country until 1960. (Courtesy of Sacramento Room, Sacramento Public Library.)

Town & Country Village was home to many specialty shops like Miles-N-Miles, Bob's Toyland, and the Clock Shop. Located at 2604 El Paseo Lane, the Clock Shop featured one of the largest clock displays on the West Coast. It is still in business today at 2630 Fulton Avenue. (Author's collection.)

Carousel Toy and Party was originally known as Bob's Toyland, which opened in 1951 in Town & Country Village. In 1981, Don and Shauna Snyder, seen here, purchased the store from original owner Bob Roberts. Its closure in 2008 was difficult for many Arden-Arcade residents, as it was an integral part of their childhood and their children's childhood, too. (Courtesy of the Center of Sacramento History.)

Teresa and Craig Higgins opened Capital Confections in Town & Country Village in 1997. Located at 2605 El Paseo Lane, the store offered a variety of chocolate delicacies and delicious gelato. One local bought his wife's Valentine's Day gifts here every year since they opened. This photograph is from the grand opening. From left to right are Alina R. Higgins, Teresa Higgins, Craig Higgins, and Marisa L. Higgins. Capital Confections closed its Town & Country location in September 2022, but offers special orders through its website. (Courtesy of Teresa and Craig Higgins.)

In 1964, the Sacramento Public Library officially opened the Arcade Branch in Town & Country Village at 2727 Marconi Avenue. This photograph is from 1970. (Courtesy of the Sacramento Room, Sacramento Public Library.)

Arcade 1 was the first fire station in Arden-Arcade and had its ground-breaking ceremony on July 12, 1942. In the background, R.L. MacDowell gives a dedication speech. Arcade 1 Station is next to Town & Country Village at 3000 Fulton Avenue. (Courtesy of Pioneer Mutual Hook and Ladder Society.)

Wayne Smith (right) was appointed Arcade's first fire chief on July 1, 1942. It was a volunteer position. Smith, seen here in 1946 receiving the brand-new Engine 2, remained chief for 12 and a half years. In October 1944, the chief and assistant chief became paid volunteer positions, with salaries of $20 a month for chief and $10 a month for assistant chief. (Courtesy of Pioneer Mutual Hook and Ladder Society.)

As the Arcade area continued to grow, so did its fire protection needs. To meet demand, the fire department offered part-time paid positions in the summer. In 1946, it purchased its first countywide radio and two gas masks. In the next several years, the fire department would see its budget and its staff grow. (Courtesy of Pioneer Mutual Hook and Ladder Society.)

Arcade firefighters participate in Fire Prevention Week festivities at Town & Country Village in the mid-1950s. Note the Village Theater in the background. (Courtesy of Pioneer Mutual Hook and Ladder Society.)

Town & Country Village was a victim of a horrific fire on November 22, 1963. A manager at Charlotte Green Apparel noticed smoke billowing from under a closet. Approximately 22,500 square feet of the shopping center were damaged. Town & Country Village was 70,000 square feet in total. (Courtesy of Pioneer Mutual Hook and Ladder Society.)

A couple of years later, on February 2, 1965, another fire wreaked havoc on Town & Country Village. Flames were seen on the roof of Big Al's Gaslite at around 3:00 a.m. The area of devastation was over 22,680 square feet. Heavily damaged stores were Phyliss Fashions, Polydor's, Marion Jensen Studio, and See's Candy. (Courtesy of Pioneer Mutual Hook and Ladder Society.)

This late 1940s–early 1950s photograph shows Jeré Strizek's famous flat-top houses. Designed with architect John W. Davis, these homes were incredibly popular due to their design and low cost. The sign reads, "Featuring Town and Country Modern Homes / Spaciously Designed and Color Coordinated for your living pleasure. . . . Economy Priced." (Courtesy of Sacramento Room, Sacramento Public Library.)

John W. Davis and Jeré Strizek won the Builders Merit Award for their modern, affordable homes. This image featured in the February 1952 issue of *Parents* magazine shows a typical Strizek and Davis kitchen with a simple layout and modern finishes. Note the stainless steel countertops. (Courtesy of Sacramento Room, Sacramento Public Library.)

Across from Town & Country Village at 2851 Fulton Avenue was the eighth location of the Stop-N-Shop supermarket chain. Seen here in 1950, it was built by the Kassis family. Additional stores in this complex were College Cleaners, Take-E-Home Chinese Food, Capco Colors Unlimited, Brownies Shop, and Hart's Pastry. (Courtesy of Sacramento Room, Sacramento Public Library.)

Fulton Avenue went from a country road to a thriving business area. This is a street scene from 1962 at the corner of Edison and Fulton Avenues looking northwest. (Courtesy of the Center of Sacramento History.)

Car lots and service centers became a large part of Fulton Avenue, which provided easy access to US Route 40 and eventually US 80. Lew Williams Chevrolet, seen here in 1964, was at 2549 Fulton Avenue near El Camino Avenue. (Courtesy of the Center of Sacramento History.)

This was the view at the corner of Edison Avenue and Fulton Avenue in 1964. Ken's Red Barn, seen in the background, opened in 1955 at 3409 Fulton Avenue. It was known for its steaks, chicken, and chops. (Courtesy of the Center of Sacramento History.)

The Coral Reef was an incredibly popular eatery in Arden-Arcade. Located at 2795 Fulton Avenue, this Polynesian-style restaurant opened in 1949. It was the destination for anniversaries, birthdays, office parties, and engagements. Residents still miss this family favorite. The Coral Reef closed in 1994. (Courtesy of the Sacramento Room, Sacramento Public Library.)

Brothers John, Elwood, and Edwin "Buddy" Maleville owned and operated the Coral Reef, seen here. They also ran the Maleville Lodge at 2712 Fulton Avenue, which was often referred to as the Coral Reef Lodge. This postcard is dated about 1965. (Courtesy of the Sacramento Room, Sacramento Public Library.)

On the left in this 1966 street scene of Watt Avenue heading north to Whitney Avenue is Raley's Supermarket, and on the right is Acme Market. (Courtesy of the Center of Sacramento History.)

Ten-year-old Dennis Trevethick and his pet fox Reddy are seen here in 1954. Trevethick lived at 3404 Maureen Drive and was given a pet fox while visiting a friend in Michigan. Three months later, Trevethick donated Reddy to the zoo at William Land Park because the fox had become unmanageable. (Courtesy of the Center of Sacramento History.)

US Route 40, also known as Auburn Boulevard, was lined with motels and inns in 1952, such as the Irish Inn, Rolling Green Inn, Town and Country Inn, and many more. The Ritz Motel was at 2228 Auburn Boulevard. Once US 80 was built, most of the motels and inns closed, and the Ritz became synonymous with crime. It was razed in the early 2000s. (Courtesy of the Sacramento Room, Sacramento Public Library.)

Clyde Derby was a premiere organ player and fixture at the Carl Greer Inn dining room at Fulton Avenue and US Route 40. Derby played the organ at various lounges and dining rooms around Sacramento. He was one of the founders of the Sierra Chapter of the American Theater Organ Society. (Courtesy of Ryan Koledin.)

Eddy's Brau Hof was one of many locations throughout the Sacramento area owned by Sam Gordon. It was a unique German-style restaurant. The location was open seven days a week until midnight, and on Fridays and Saturdays until 3:00 a.m. This location was conveniently right off US Routes 40 and 80. (Courtesy of Ryan Koledin.)

Five

MEMBERS-ONLY CLUB

Members-only clubs are a part of the framework of Arden-Arcade. They are part of the identity of this community. Three of these clubs have received numerous accolades for their athletic feats and epic festivities, which have brought media attention to the community. These clubs are still active and thriving today.

Del Paso Country Club was the first and oldest club in Arden-Arcade. Established in 1916, it is still considered one of the premier golfing locations in the Sacramento region and the country. It has continually upgraded and redesigned its golf course to keep the club active and relevant in the golfing community. Additionally, Del Paso Country Club has hosted celebrity golf tournaments and member barbecues and carried on the tradition of night putting.

The Arden Hills Tennis and Swimming Club was founded in 1954 by Sherm Chavoor, a world-renowned Olympic swimming coach. The Arden district was very rural at the time Arden Hills opened, but soon it attracted national attention because of its athletic achievements. Swim meets and tennis matches became media spectacles. Today, Arden Hills Tennis and Swimming Club is simply known as Arden Hills. Over the years, it has rebranded itself as an exclusive luxury wellness retreat offering members high-end amenities that include its Olympic-sized swimming pool.

The Del Norte Club opened in 1957 and was tucked away in the Del Norte Woods neighborhood a few blocks from Del Paso Country Club. Like Arden Hills, Del Norte was known primarily for tennis and swimming. Del Norte athletes were known for breaking records and being formidable opponents. Moreover, Del Norte was known for its fantastic parties. Today, the club is an active, well-maintained, and popular family-friendly fitness center.

This 1925 photograph shows Del Paso Country Club, which was established in 1916 by John L. Black; the property was once used as a pathway through the Sierra Mountains. (Courtesy of Sacramento Room, Sacramento Public Library.)

The Del Paso Clubhouse, built in 1916, is seen here in 1929. The interior featured oak furniture and Oriental tapestries. There was a lounge area for men and women. The clubhouse also offered billiard tables, an outdoor swimming pool, and a bowling alley. (Courtesy of Sacramento Room, Sacramento Public Library.)

This Del Paso Country Club youth class photograph from 1929 features golf professional Frank Minch, at far right. Minch held junior golf clinics at Del Paso until his retirement in 1965. (Courtesy of Sacramento Room, Sacramento Public Library.)

Del Paso Country Club has continually updated, redesigned, and improved the club. This photograph from 1929 shows the unveiling of a new swimming pool, part of a $23,000 improvement plan for the club. (Courtesy of Sacramento Room, Sacramento Public Library.)

This is a 1938 aerial photograph of Del Country Club. North of the club, on Marconi and Fulton Avenues, is the future location of Town & Country Village. To the right of this location is the outline of new home developments next to Pope Avenue. (Courtesy of the Center of Sacramento History.)

Del Paso Country Club hosts an annual charity event called Swing at Cancer, which attracted many notable figures, including film star and director Clint Eastwood, seen here in 1977 signing autographs for fans after the sixth-annual charity golf game. (Courtesy of the Center of Sacramento History.)

Comedian and movie star Bob Hope also attended the charity event in 1977, along with musician Lawrence Welk. Standing behind Hope is professional golfer Johnny Miller. (Courtesy of the Center of Sacramento History.)

This 1961 photograph shows the parking lot of the Arden Hills club looking roughly southeast down Mission Avenue toward Fair Oaks Boulevard. Arden Hills was established in 1954 by swim coach Sherm Chavoor. (Courtesy of the Vedanta Society.)

When Arden Hills first opened, the primary focus was to create a training facility for swimming and tennis athletes. This photograph from the early 1960s shows packed stands for a swim meet. Arden Hills would soon become nationally known for its Olympic swimmers. (Courtesy of Arden Hills.)

Sherm Chavoor, seen here with Olympic gold medalist Mark Spitz, became world famous for his ability to train Olympic swimmers. His Arden Hills swimmers earned 31 Olympic medals—20 of which were gold. (Courtesy of Arden Hills.)

Arden Hills was a premiere tennis training facility and was known for its tennis tournaments, too. Usually, the female competitions would be at Arden Hills and the male competitions at Del Norte. This photograph is from around the 1960s. (Courtesy of Arden Hills.)

Tennis legend Jim Nelson is seen here in 1977 at the Del Norte Club. The Del Norte Club is located at 3040 Becerra Way and has been an Arden-Arcade establishment since 1957. (Courtesy of the Center of Sacramento History.)

Del Norte is not only known for its athletic facilities, but also as a legendary party place. It hosted a poolside fashion show and dessert party in 1958, as well as a Hawaiian luau. Today, the club is a community fitness hub for families. (Author's collection.)

Six

ALL ABOUT ARDEN

Although Arden-Arcade is a hyphenated name, it does contain two separate districts, according to the old fire department records. The Arcade fire district was officially established in 1942, and the Arden fire district became official in 1943. However, researching through historical records, the two districts have tended to be linked and named together in various media. Studying a map of Arden-Arcade after the annexation of California Exposition, Arden Fair, Campus Commons, and Haggin Oaks, it appears the Arcade district was everything north of Cottage Way between Ethan Way and Mission Avenue, and the Arden district was south of Cottage Way and between the above-mentioned streets, ending at the American River. Arden-Arcade's boundaries have fluctuated over the years, and at some point, the eastern boundary was as far as Walnut Avenue. Perhaps the area was so rural back at the time, it was just easier to include both names when giving directions. Then when talk of incorporation began, both names were used. Whatever the reason, there are two distinct vibes when traveling through this diverse community.

Arden was one step behind Arcade in development, and remained rural longer, as Arcade developed rapidly with the opening of Town & Country Village in 1946. The Arden Town Shopping Center did not open until 1948. Arden's big development boom happened in the 1960s due to Arden Fair, California Exposition, the expansion of Watt Avenue Bridge, and the construction of the Howe Avenue Bridge. Arden has neighborhoods like Arden Oaks that are tucked away between two busy main routes, Watt and Eastern Avenues. This hidden gem transports visitors to a delightful little forested hideaway in this sprawling metropolis, where one will likely be greeted by a rafter of wild turkeys. Additionally, Arden has dealt with devastating floods from the American River, most notably the flood of 1950. The levees broke due to excessive rain in November and again in December 1950. Though Arden and Arcade may have started out as separate districts, they have had to lean on one another during catastrophic events like floods and fires.

1948

WATT

ARDEN

This 1948 aerial photograph shows the intersections of Watt Avenue and Arden Way. Arden School is on the southeast corner of the intersection. Before Arden School was built in 1914, children would attend school under an oak tree across the street, the site of a Rite Aid today. (Courtesy of Arden Middle School.)

The intersection of Watt Avenue and Fair Oaks Boulevard is seen here in 1949. La Sierra Drive curves at center, with only a handful of homes dotting the landscape. Fair Oaks Boulevard and Watt Avenue were only two-lane roads at this time. (Courtesy of Donald Cox.)

Arden Town Shopping Center, at the intersection of Watt Avenue and Fair Oaks Boulevard, is seen here in 1948 with the Arden Variety store and Arden Town appliance and hardware store. Arden Town was a $200,000 project as part of a community plan designed for Wright and Kimbrough

This photograph was taken on April 17, 1948, by Eugene Hepting shortly after the Cardinal Market opened at Arden Town Shopping Center. The first manager was 27-year-old Ted Foster, the youngest manager in the history of Cardinal Market at the time. His assistant was 21-year-old Ray Drisdell. The market was considered ultra-modern and built by Wright and Kimbrough. (Courtesy of the Center of Sacramento History.)

by Will G. Norris. Barovetti and Thomas were the architects, and C.C. Ruby was the builder. (Courtesy of the Center of Sacramento History.)

Watt Avenue Bridge, seen here in 1956, was low and narrow. Children used it as a diving platform to cool off from the summer heat. In 1959, the county began constructing an automobile bridge after settling a land ownership dispute with Carl Selby. (Courtesy of the Center of Sacramento History.)

Eugene Hepting poses on the Watt Avenue Bridge on January 8, 1961. In 1960, the bridge was officially closed to automobiles during construction; however, it was still open for pedestrian and horse traffic. (Courtesy of the Center of Sacramento History.)

The intersection of Fulton Avenue and Sierra Boulevard is pictured in 1938. The dirt road that heads into the orchard is today's Munroe Avenue. In the foreground is a sign for chiropractor Dr. P.R. Mandeville and a mailbox for A.J. Argante. (Courtesy of Sacramento Room, Sacramento Public Library.)

Eugene Hepting took this photograph of a small farm on the west side of Fulton Avenue near Hurley Avenue on November 16, 1947. In 1932, Hurley Avenue had only five residents. (Courtesy of the Center of Sacramento History.)

Fair Oaks Boulevard and Fulton Avenue are underwater in 1950. There were two levee breaches along the American River, which caused widespread flooding. The Oaks restaurant is seen at center. (Courtesy of the Center of Sacramento History.)

The H Street Bridge over the American River is seen here during the flood. The levee breaches resulted in hundreds of rescues over the weekend of November 19, 1950. Mr. and Mrs. Frank Jones of Memory Lane, just west of Fulton Avenue, woke up at 5:00 a.m. to a foot of water in their bedroom. They quickly escaped, and by daylight, their car and house were underwater. (Courtesy of the Center of Sacramento History.)

During the 1950 flood, the water reached the street signs, as seen in this Eugene Hepting photograph taken at the corner of Howe Avenue and Fair Oaks Boulevard. (Courtesy of the Center of Sacramento History.)

Eugene Hepting photographed his wife and dog Fritzie standing near a large pile of manure swept in by flood near the Howe and Arden Service station. The flood current was so strong that one person, who lived at 580 Howe Avenue, had a ring in a closed bureau drawer in the bedroom that ended up in a furnace vent in the living room. (Courtesy of the Center of Sacramento History.)

Arden Fair is seen from the air in the late 1950s. Arden Way is at center. In the foreground are Howe Avenue and cattle grazing pastures. Arden Fair was originally an outdoor shopping center much like Town & Country Village. It was converted into an indoor mall in 1969. (Courtesy of the Center of Sacramento History.)

Arden Way is seen looking west toward US 80 in the 1950s. On the left is a farm with a barn behind what appears to be a line of eucalyptus trees. Shoppers regularly saw cattle and sheep grazing across the street from Arden Fair. (Courtesy of the Center of Sacramento History.)

The new Sears store is under construction in 1956, the first building built for the new Arden Fair. Developers were William Gannon and Philip F. Heraty with Kassis Investment Company. (Courtesy of the Center of Sacramento History.)

The new Sears was built on 30 acres of Swanston Estates. Seen here in 1956, was the first of many retail stores to be built on an additional 100 acres. Others were Stop-N-Shop, FW Woolworth, Gallenkamp shoes, and Lane Bryant, which still occupies its original location from 1962. (Courtesy of the Center of Sacramento History.)

Frank Kassis points at the future home of Arden Fair in 1956. Kassis was president of the Kassis Investment Company, which leased the land from developers Philip F. Heraty and William Gannon. Additionally, he was the general manager/owner of the Stop-N-Shop stores throughout the Sacramento region. (Courtesy of the Center of Sacramento History.)

From left to right around 1956 are Kassis brothers Lew, Ed, Frank, John, and Walter. All were involved in the investment business, except for John, who was a doctor in Midtown, although he was known to be a silent investor. The Kassis brothers made a name from themselves as developers of Country Club Lanes, Country Club Plaza, Stop-N-Shop supermarkets, and Arden Fair. (Courtesy of the Center of Sacramento History.)

This 1956 lithograph from architecture firm Dreyfuss + Blackford shows the future Arden Fair. The Kassis brothers' concept of the Food Circus was a precursor to the mall food court. On the left is Thrifty, and at far right is Stop-N-Shop and Cork and Bottle. Frank Kassis was a savvy networker, and his relationships with retailers were one of the main keys to success for Arden Fair. (Courtesy of the Center of Sacramento History.)

This 1958 photograph shows the Sacramento Inn complex at 1401 Arden Way, northwest of Sears at Arden Fair. The Sacramento Inn was estimated to cost $5 million to construct. The complex contained 500 rooms, a 24,000-square-foot restaurant, a swimming pool, a nine-hole pitch and putt golf course, and the Starlite drive-in theater. (Courtesy of the Center of Sacramento History.)

The Alta Arden Expressway was officially christened on September 22, 1970. This aerial photograph shows the intersection of Arden Way, Ethan Way, and Exposition Boulevard. The expressway was controversial at the time, as councilmembers and engineers looked at ways to connect the newly constructed California Exposition to existing infrastructure. (Courtesy of the Center of Sacramento History.)

Fantasia Mini Golf was at 3421 Arden Way. There was also a section called Funland that offered go-karts, a jet slide, a funhouse, a birthday party house, and billiards. Owner Dan Benvenuti ran into some controversy in 1974 when his establishment was picketed by local Asian high school clubs for using signs that contained negative and offensive stereotypes of Asian Americans. He ultimately removed the signs. (Courtesy of Ryan Koledin.)

Miller's Drive-in, at Watt Avenue and Arden Way, was a chain burger joint and had locations in Rio Linda and North Highlands. In 1956, they released two new burgers: the Miller's Deluxe for 35¢ and the Miller's Supreme for 45¢. This location is pictured in 1955. (Courtesy of the Center of Sacramento History.)

This advertisement for Arden Park Vista was prepared by real estate developers Wright and Kimbrough in 1940. In the background, Town & Country Village has not been built except for Jeré Strizek's Bohemian Village, and most of the Arden-Arcade area is undeveloped. (Courtesy of Sacramento Room, Sacramento Public Library.)

At a party at a Sierra Oaks Vista home, architect Mary Barden sits at left. Barden was the architect of many homes in Sierra Oaks and Sierra Oaks Vista. She was the architect for Sherm Chavoor's home, the owner of Arden Hills Tennis and Swimming Club. She and her husband, John, subdivided Carlotta Heights in Carmichael and designed and built homes in the Wilhaggin area. (Courtesy of Stephanie Barden.)

John Barden (left) was a builder and husband of architect Mary Barden, stepson of Frank "Squeaky" Williams. Squeaky was a prominent architect in East Sacramento, Del Dayo, and Land Park. John Barden began building in the Sacramento area in 1916. (Courtesy of Stephanie Barden.)

This late 1940s–early 1950s photograph shows Arden Fire Department trucks lined up in a neighborhood, likely Arden Park. The Arden Fire Department become official on January 4, 1943. Prior to this, there was a group of local citizens who called themselves the Sierra Oaks Fire Protection League. (Courtesy of Pioneer Mutual Hook and Ladder Society.)

84

Jamie Gray of 891 Los Molinos Way in Arden Park plays on his toy horse in his backyard in 1953. In the background are a garden and a pet duck. (Courtesy of Dan Jensen.)

SAC Neighborhoods - Arden

Arden Park
VISTA

Offers You--

A BETTER WAY OF LIVING
Country life with all its beauty, peace and freedom, combined with convenience.

SPACE AND PRIVACY
Individual homesites range from approximately one-quarter acre to one acre, or more, in the heart of the great Rancho Del Paso.

ARCHITECTURAL CONTROL
This all-embracing common sense control guarantees buildings and improvements in harmony with the surroundings.

SCHOOL FACILITIES
Arden Park Vista enjoys the facility of the Arden Elementary School and the Grant Union High School which have school busses available practically at your front door.

RECREATIONAL ADVANTAGES
The Del Paso and Municipal Golf Courses are adjacent and are easily accessible. Horseback riding in the country is another sport to enjoy. There is ample room for swimming pools, barbecues and all types of outdoor living.

A COUNTRY HOME
Within easy reach of your city office. Only six miles or 15 minutes from 10th and K.

WRIGHT & KIMBROUGH
819 J STREET • DIAL 2-2991

This Arden Park Vista brochure was produced by developers Wright and Kimbrough in the 1950s. It lists all the amenities Arden Park Vista offered a potential home buyer, from space and privacy to recreational activities. (Courtesy of Sacramento Room. Sacramento Public Library.)

Jamie Gray is seen again with his mother, Kathryn, and their pup. Kathryn was the original owner of the Arden Park home. She purchased the land and had the quintessential California ranch home built. (Courtesy of Dan Jensen.)

This photograph was taken around 1958 during a summer pool party in the backyard of a home on Windsor Drive in Arden Manor. From left to right are (first row, in pool) Jim, Livia, and Melinda; (second row) parents Jim Alberti and Madeline Alberti, with Jim's sister Inez and Diane Alberti. (Courtesy of Melinda Alberti Jung.)

This c. 1966 photograph shows a 1958 Thunderbird cruising around Arden Manor. In the front seat from left to right are Bonita Moser (driver), Kevin Fenno, and Bob Edgar. In the back seat are Cris Connolly, Mindy Alberti, Terry Moser, and John Mulkins. (Courtesy of Melinda Alberti Jung.)

The 1959 Arden Park Little League all-star team won its first game against Roseville but lost the next night to the Auburn team. From left to right are (first row) Coach Geandrot, Jack Stansfield, Jimmy Olson, Allan Davis, John Fuller, Bobby Geandrot, Warren Bernoff, and Coach Drennan; (second row) Danny Segalis, Jeff Boroski, Chuck Cusack, Ric Williams, Rick Niello, Gary Foster, Eric French, and Don Murphy. (Courtesy of Ric Williams.)

This c. 1969 aerial photograph shows the Campus Commons and Sierra Oaks areas of Arden-Arcade. At far left is the H Street Bridge, followed by the Guy A. West Bridge, a pedestrian-only bridge built in 1968, then the Howe Avenue Bridge under construction, and the Watt Avenue Bridge at far right. (Courtesy of the Sacramento Country Day School.)

In 1964, a group of Sacramento Country Day School students climb trees at the school's original site at the Unitarian Universalist campus on Sierra Boulevard. The school moved to Latham Drive in September 1965. (Courtesy of the Sacramento Country Day School.)

Beloved teacher Frank Pignata and his sixth-grade class from Sacramento Country Day School cross the Guy A. West Bridge after a 1966 class trip to Sacramento State University. (Courtesy of the Sacramento Country Day School.)

A young boy dressed as a sailor participates in a Halloween event at Arden School in the 1950s. The school's enrollment hovered at less than 300 pupils until the early 1950s, when it dramatically increased due to the affordability of land and all the new businesses in the area. (Courtesy of Arden Middle School.)

Arden School youngsters are dressed up for Halloween in the 1950s. During World War II, Arden School was a community hub where dozens of residents would gather in the auditorium to discuss ways to help the war effort or to express concerns. (Courtesy of Arden Middle School.)

Children take a joyous wagon ride in the 1960s. Wagon rides were a nod to Arden School's roots, as the school developed in 1914. Thirty-five families relocated to the area from Oklahoma and purchased tracts for farming near the school. They planned to turn their community into a "little Oklahoma." (Courtesy of Arden Middle School.)

The Arden-Dimick Library is at 891 Watt Avenue. The architect for this unique building was Nicholas A. Tomich. The Arden branch officially opened in 1972 and has remained a community staple. It is seen here around 1980. (Courtesy of the Sacramento Room, Sacramento Public Library.)

The Arden-Dimick library expanded in 1998, due to the generosity of Dr. Max Dimick and his wife, Nadine. Dr. Dimick was a doctor in Sacramento and delivered over 5,000 babies. Nadine was a nurse, and both were members of the Del Paso Country Club. The Dimick family donated $800,000 to the library expansion project. Max and Nadine lived in the Sacramento area for over five decades. (Courtesy of the Sacramento Room, Sacramento Public Library.)

Pictured in 1959, this property at 2425 Sierra Boulevard was the new building site for the Unitarian Universalist Church. Along Sierra Boulevard were windmills pumping irrigation water for crops. The road itself was very narrow and sparsely populated. (Courtesy of the Unitarian Universalist Society of Sacramento.)

The ground-breaking ceremony for the Unitarian Universalist church on Sierra Boulevard was on August 23, 1959. The residential and business boom in Arden-Arcade in the 1950s included the growth of faith centers. (Courtesy of the Unitarian Universalist Society of Sacramento.)

A dedicated member of the Unitarian Universalist church poses at the construction site at 2425 Sierra Boulevard in 1959. The architect was John Harvey Carter, who built the Arcade Library at 2443 Marconi Avenue. The walls of the church had cuts that would be filled with glass to provide a view of the garden. (Courtesy of the Unitarian Universalist Society of Sacramento.)

This was the future site of the Vedanta Society of Sacramento, at 1337 Mission Avenue, around 1950. The Sacramento center of Vedanta was a branch of the San Francisco Temple. Swami Ashokananda oversaw the construction of the new monastery. (Courtesy of the Vedanta Society of Sacramento.)

Swami Ashokananda speaks with a worker at the new Vedanta center. The building was designed by architect Henry Gutterson of San Francisco. Many monks worked here throughout the year and lived in tents on the property until the chapel was completed in 1953. (Courtesy of the Vedanta Society of Sacramento.)

The chapel is under construction around 1950. Thirteen years after this photograph, a permanent temple, auditorium, library, and other offices were added to the property. (Courtesy of Vedanta Society of Sacramento.)

The Vedanta Society was originally named the Church of Universal Philosophy and Religion, changing its name in 1970. This 1960s photograph shows part of the lush gardens on the Vedanta Society property. Today, the society is known for its serene gardens. (Courtesy of Vedanta Society of Sacramento.)

This aerial photograph shows how developed the Arden-Arcade area is in recent times. In the foreground is Arden Middle School. Toward the center and foreground are Country Club Centre and Country Club Plaza. In the distance is Del Paso Country Club. (Courtesy of Arden Middle School.)

Seven

MID-CENTURY MARVELS

When someone mentions a city, usually it conjures up an iconic structure that defines part of the city's identity. For example, Seattle, Washington, is home to the Space Needle. Built in 1962, the structure was part of the architectural style known as Googie, which originated in Southern California. The design was considered ultra-modern at the time and was inspired by the space age and popular imagery such as in the cartoon *The Jetsons*. Features include hyperbolic paraboloids, upswept roofs, geometric shapes, symbols suggesting motion, and shapes representing things like flying saucers. Googie architecture is included in the Mid-century Modern movement, which started around 1945 and lasted until 1970. Arden-Arcade is fortunate to have some remaining Googie structures, as well as other Mid-century Modern marvels.

Arden-Arcade is also lucky to have structures designed by world-renowned architects. The Weinstocks-Lubin/Macy's building in Country Club Plaza was designed by architect Charles Luckman. Some of his many notable California designs are the Forum (now Kia Forum) in Inglewood and the Theme Building at Los Angeles International Airport, a notable Googie structure.

Architecture can make one community aesthetically distinct from another, and its preservation can bring future tourist traffic. An added benefit is that it allows for memories of a space to continue as people visit and feel the energy. Arden-Arcade's architectural marvels served a function, but at the same time facilitated an experience.

Country Club Lanes bowling alley is under construction around 1959. The design includes hyperbolic and parabolic features on the main entrance. Designed by Powers, Daly, and De Rosa, Country Club Lanes offered a coffee shop, banquet rooms, and billiards along with 48 bowling lanes. It is still in business today. (Courtesy of the Center of Sacramento History.)

Safeway grocery store opened in 1966 at 2509 Fulton Avenue. The building is designed with Googie architecture that encompasses style elements such as exaggeration and dramatic angles. Note how the roof pitches with extreme flair. Today, Tognotti's Auto World occupies this iconic building. (Courtesy of the Center of Sacramento History.)

Sam's Big Top coffee shop opened in 1966 at 2721 El Camino Avenue. It was designed by Armet and Davis with local architect Sooky Lee supervising the construction. This is another Googie structure in Arden-Arcade. In July 2016, as a beloved breakfast diner named Flapjacks, the building suffered a catastrophic fire; however, owner Frank Tofanelli rebuilt the structure with the original blueprints, resurrecting and preserving this local landmark. (Courtesy of the Center of Sacramento History.)

The Kassis family was well known for their Stop-N-Shop supermarkets, with 12 throughout the Sacramento area. This one was at 1120 El Camino Avenue. The structure had elements of Googie architecture, but is now lost. (Courtesy of the Center of Sacramento History.)

White Front department store at 3400 Arden Way is seen here in 1964. The discount store opened in August of that year. White Front was a chain store based in Los Angeles, and the Arden store was part of an expansion to Northern California. It featured a hyperbolic and parabolic design over the main entrance. It is a lost Mid-century marvel. (Courtesy of the Center of Sacramento History.)

On the corner of Fulton and El Camino Avenues stood Harvey's Drive-In, a trendy destination for teenagers in the 1960s. Many would cruise the downtown loop on K Street and end up at Harvey's on Fulton Avenue. The restaurant is unfortunately lost. (Courtesy of Dreyfuss + Blackford.)

Sambo's Pancakes was at 3140 Arden Way and is another lost Mid-century marvel. Sambo's was a chain breakfast joint that began in Santa Barbara, California. The theme was based on the book *The Story of Little Black Sambo*, which contained offensive caricatures of Black indigenous people. The name is now considered a derogatory term. The last remaining Sambo's, in Santa Barbara, officially changed its name to Chad's in 2020. (Courtesy of Ryan Koledin.)

Eggie's restaurant is a Googie structure that is still standing at 1650 Fulton Avenue. Eggie's was another legendary breakfast location. After 40 years in business, the restaurant closed due to the COVID-19 pandemic; however, the Toasted Rooster Café opened in 2022 and is carrying on the breakfast diner tradition. (Author's collection.)

Lyon's Coffee Shop was on the corner of El Camino and Watt Avenues. This 1966 photograph shows the Weinstocks building in the background. Lyon's was built by Erickson Construction Co., and the architect was Edward Wong. This Lyon's location closed in 2004, and the building was razed in 2007. (Courtesy of the Center of Sacramento History.)

This is the courtyard of the Pacific Telephone headquarters at 2700 Watt Avenue, which opened in 1963. This unique building was designed by Wayne Solomon Hertzka and William Howard Knowles. (Courtesy of the Center of Sacramento History.)

Fey's Hardware was on the corner of La Sierra Drive and Fair Oaks Boulevard in Arden Town shopping center. It was designed by architects Dreyfuss + Blackford in 1953. Owner George J. Fey closed the store in 1961 and moved to Montana to take up cattle ranching. (Courtesy of Dreyfuss + Blackford.)

Landmark Business and Financial Center is pictured when new in 1985. The unique structure was designed by Leason Pomeroy Association. The $24 million facility includes 180,000 square feet and is one of many exceptional architectural buildings in Arden-Arcade. (Courtesy of the Center of Sacramento History.)

Local architect John Harvey Carter designed and built the new location for the Arcade Library at 2443 Marconi Avenue. Its unique sunken, earth-berm design was intended to muffle traffic noise from cars and aircraft flying over from McClellan Air Force Base. This photograph is from 1976. (Courtesy of the Sacramento Room, Sacramento Public Library.)

This was the interior of the Arcade Library in 1976. John Harvey Carter used skylights to maximize natural lighting in the space, and large windows to look out onto courtyards. The design was intended to encourage people to connect with nature. (Courtesy of Sacramento Room, Sacramento Public Library.)

Best Products Co., at the east end of Arden Fair, caused quite a stir with its quirky entry. Seen here in 1977, the design gives the impression that the building has been ripped apart. The detached portion of the wall was mounted on rails and could roll open and closed with the push of a button. Onlookers gathered at the grand opening to see the "wandering wall," as the builders called it, in action. (Courtesy of the Center of Sacramento History.)

Originally built as a Weinstock-Lubin store for Country Club Plaza in 1960, this building eventually become a Macy's department store in 1995. The structure was designed by world-renowned architect Charles Luckman of Los Angeles. One of Luckman's most famous designs is the Forum (now Kia Forum) indoor arena in Inglewood. Arden-Arcade is lucky to have one of his designs. (Courtesy of Gretchen Steinberg.)

Eight

COUNTRY CLUB CITY

George Zwirkis, affectionately known to locals as the "Goatman," was seen all over Arden-Arden with his herd of goats roaming the open grassland. He was an offbeat character who was well-known to early settlers and developers. He owned 24 acres at the northwest corner of Cottage Way and Watt Avenue, where he lived in a small shack with his goats and was known as a jovial neighbor who knew all the news. Originally from Greece, Zwirkis arrived in Sacramento around 1924 and worked as a sheepherder for the Swanstons, until he left to become a goat rancher. When Country Club Centre was built in 1952, Zwirkis apparently loved it and would stop by frequently to get coffee and doughnuts. In 1956, Zwirkis sold his property for $156,000 and moved to Elk Grove with his goats. He passed away shortly after, but his legend lives on.

Once Country Club Centre was built, it was only a matter of time before the other three corners of El Camino and Watt Avenues were developed. Zwirkis's departure from the area represents this shift from goat fields to retail. By the early 1960s, the area was dubbed by advertisers as "Country Club City." The sheer volume of stores available at the time was incredible. A student at Country Club Beauty School, which was behind Tower Records, said, "After school, we would hop over to Tower Records and go to Sam's Hof Brau for a bite to eat, or we would go bowling at Country Lanes." During the 1970s and 1980s, Weinstocks and Country Club Plaza hosted numerous events, such as a needlepoint class with movie star Sylvia Sidney and local high school orchestral concerts. Today, Country Club Plaza hosts a popular farmer's market.

Although Arden-Arcade technically does not have a downtown corridor, if one was to be chosen, Country Club City would likely be the best candidate. It connects both the Arcade and Arden districts, and it is centrally located. One resident quipped, "The vacant Weinstocks-Lubin building would make a great city hall!"

Country Club Centre is pictured in 1952. In the foreground is the future site of Country Club Plaza. Construction began on the site in December 1948. It originally had a movie theater named Centre Theater operated by Joseph Blumenfeld, who ran several theaters in Sacramento. However, the movie house was not a part of the final design. (Courtesy of the Center of Sacramento History.)

A car show is in progress in the Country Club Centre parking lot in 1958. In the foreground, in front of Emigh Hardware and W.T. Grant Co., a band is playing. Country Club Centre was designed by architect William B. David of San Francisco. The shopping center was built on 20 acres, with room for expansion. (Courtesy of Sacramento Room, Sacramento Public Library.)

The Country Club Centre parking lot lis seen in 1952 looking northeast toward the intersection of Watt and El Camino Avenues. At the time, there were only about 1,000 residents in Arden-Arcade. Country Club Centre was named after Del Paso Country Club. (Courtesy of Sacramento Room, Sacramento Public Library.)

Emigh Hardware is an Arden-Arcade landmark. The store is beloved by the community, as it has been a longstanding retailer with outstanding customer service. This photograph was taken around 1952, shortly after Country Club Centre opened for business. (Courtesy of Emigh Hardware.)

James Emigh (pictured) and his brother Clay opened Emigh Hardware in 1908 at 1208 J Street. In 1912, the company merged with retailers Winchell and Cline and the business moved to 310 J Street, and again to Seventh and J Streets. (Courtesy of Emigh Hardware.)

The inside of Emigh Hardware's 310 J Street location is seen here in 1922. Note the ladder used to reach inventory on the high, well-stocked shelves. (Courtesy of Emigh Hardware.)

Colby Emigh was responsible for bringing Emigh to Arden-Arcade. As the postwar building boom took hold in Arden-Arcade, he took a risk and moved the store to what he considered "the country." (Courtesy of Emigh Hardware.)

Shortly after moving to Arden-Arcade, Emigh Hardware, seen here in 1958, created a cartoon of pigtailed girls in overalls saying, "Call me Amy," as many locals had a difficult time pronouncing the name Emigh. The character was based on Colby and Jesma Emigh's daughters Carol and Mary. (Courtesy of Emigh Hardware.)

Colby Emigh's son-in-law Rich Lawrence took over Emigh Ace Hardware in 1971. In 1973, he moved the store from Country Club Centre to its current location, 3555 El Camino Avenue. The store has expanded to include Emigh's Outdoor Living in 2000, which was managed by Rich's son Brian Lawrence, who is continuing the family legacy. In 2022, Emigh opened a second location in El Dorado Hills. (Courtesy of Emigh Hardware.)

Frank Kassis's family stands on the future site of Country Club Plaza between El Camino Avenue and Butano Drive on Watt Avenue in October 1957. Developed by Earl Cohen of Beverly Hills, the shopping center opened in 1961. One of its unique features was Gourmet Lane. (Courtesy of the Center of Sacramento History.)

The newly opened Gallenkamps shoe store in Country Club Plaza is pictured in 1961. Gallenkamps had over 500 locations nationwide. Other chain department stores in the mall were Marlene's, Florsheim Shoes, and Parklane Hosiery. (Courtesy of the Center of Sacramento History.)

An evening event is taking place at Weinstocks-Lubin department store in Country Club Plaza in 1961. The exterior walls on the first floor are made of Portuguese marble. In the interior, Tennessee pink marble was used in the central area of the first floor, and Alabama cream marble was used on vertical portions of the escalators. (Courtesy of the Center of Sacramento History.)

The new basement café in the Weinstocks-Lubin department store in Country Club Plaza was busy in 1978. The café was part of a $1.5 million project to revitalize the store. The basement was named the Pavilion and included imported housewares, luggage, and other goods. (Courtesy of the Center of Sacramento History.)

Actress Sylvia Sidney stopped by Weinstock at Country Club Plaza to showcase her needlepoint kits and to teach a needlepoint class in 1971. Weinstock was also visited by actor Kelly Ward, who played Putzie in the movie *Grease* in 1978. He autographed photographs in the juniors department and attended a screening of the movie with fans at Capitol Theatres at 2842 Watt Avenue. (Courtesy of the Center of Sacramento History.)

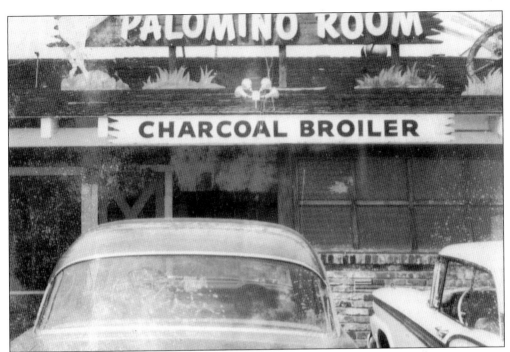

This was the original front of the Palomino Room at the corner of El Camino and Yorktown Avenues in 1956. The Palomino Room was owned and operated by brothers Ray Boroski (Ray dropped the "w" in his last name by accident when he joined the Army) and Harry Borowski. Ray initially opened a television and appliance store at this location in 1954, but at the urging of his brother, who ran a nightclub in Ohio, the two embarked on a restaurant and lounge. (Courtesy of Debbie Viramontes.)

The Palomino Room sign from El Camino Avenue is seen here around 1970. Underneath is a sign for Jack's House of Music at 2528 Yorktown Avenue, a popular music store that opened in 1956. It was owned by musician E. Norton "Jack" Hyde. Many locals bought their first guitars and drum sets at Jack's. This location closed in 2002 and is still greatly missed by the residents of Arden-Arcade. (Courtesy of Debbie Viramontes.)

The Palomino Bottle Shop is pictured in 1973. Ray Boroski and Harry Borowski purchased the entire corner of El Camino and Yorktown Avenues in the early 1970s. In 1988, the Bottle Shop became part of the front dining room after a renovation. (Courtesy of Debbie Viramontes.)

In front of the iconic golden horses above the piano bar in the Palomino Room are Ray's grandson Bryan Boroski in front, with (from left to right) Ray's daughters Cathy, Carol, and Debbie, and Ray's wife, Stella. The Palomino was known for great service, delicious food, and good times. It was a difficult loss for the community when it closed in 1999. (Courtesy of Debbie Viramontes.)

Sam's Hof Brau was an Arden-Arcade favorite since 1959. Located at 2500 Watt Avenue, Sam's, seen here in 1996, was next door to Tower Records, and behind the restaurant was Country Club Beauty School. On February 7, 2023, a devasting fire caused extensive damage to the restaurant's interior. Many residents, employees, and former employees are still reeling from this tragedy. (Courtesy of the Sacramento Room, Sacramento Public Library.)

At one time, there were a variety of shops next to Sam's Hof Brau, Tower Records, and Tower Books. At far left in this early 1970s view of El Camino Avenue is Country Club Lanes bowling alley. (Courtesy of the Center of Sacramento History.)

Tower Records founder Russell Solomon sets up the first standalone store at 2514 Watt Avenue around 1960. Solomon began selling records out of his father's drugstore in downtown Sacramento. Note the cash register set up on sawhorse tables. (Courtesy of the Center of Sacramento History.)

A former Tower employee noted the diversity of Arden-Arcade customers' purchases, which ranged from classical to jazz and rock-n-roll. Many young residents would spend hours in the listening booths playing new 45s and albums. The store is seen here around 1967. (Courtesy of the Center of Sacramento History.)

Buck Owens and Susan Raye play a free concert in the Tower Records parking lot in 1970. Note the folks on the roof. Russell Solomon was known to book musical acts around town and host free shows in the Watt Avenue parking lot. (Courtesy of the Center of Sacramento History.)

Tower Records at Watt Avenue is busy in 1970. The store not only offered the latest releases, but also sold plants, posters, pottery, candles, patches, tarot cards, and much more—even blacklights. (Courtesy of the Center of Sacramento History.)

The staff of Tower Video on Watt Avenue poses for a fun holiday card in the late 1980s–early 1990s. The store both rented and sold videos. Those who grew up in the area hold immense nostalgia for the original Tower Records. (Courtesy of the Center of Sacramento History.)

In June 1996, Metallica played a free concert in front of Tower Records on Watt Avenue even though they did not secure a permit. This was part of the band's promotional tour for the album *Load*. (Courtesy of the Center of Sacramento History.)

Over 3,000 people showed up to see Metallica perform on the back of a flatbed truck in the parking lot. The concert began around 9:30 p.m. and lasted 30 minutes, with the crowd wildly cheering. (Courtesy of the Center of Sacramento History.)

Metallica guitarist Kirk Hammett plays as security keeps the rowdy crowd from encroaching on the stage. It was a memorable summer night, and a reminder of the cultural impact Tower Records had on the area and the world. (Courtesy of the Center of Sacramento History.)

The rapid development of Arden-Arcade since the opening of Country Club Centre in 1952 is quite evident in this aerial view of the intersection of Watt and El Camino Avenues and surrounding areas just 10 years later. (Courtesy of the Center of Sacramento History.)

DISCOVER THOUSANDS OF LOCAL HISTORY BOOKS FEATURING MILLIONS OF VINTAGE IMAGES

Arcadia Publishing, the leading local history publisher in the United States, is committed to making history accessible and meaningful through publishing books that celebrate and preserve the heritage of America's people and places.

Find more books like this at
www.arcadiapublishing.com

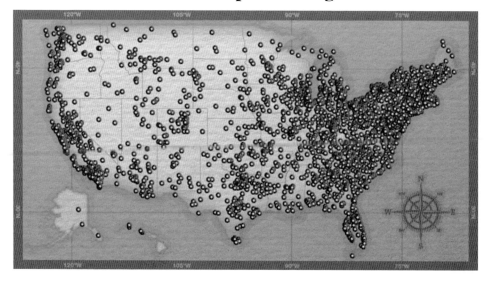

Search for your hometown history, your old stomping grounds, and even your favorite sports team.

Consistent with our mission to preserve history on a local level, this book was printed in South Carolina on American-made paper and manufactured entirely in the United States. Products carrying the accredited Forest Stewardship Council (FSC) label are printed on 100 percent FSC-certified paper.

MADE IN THE